Manufactured by Amazon.ca
Bolton, ON

15259415R00057